THIS BOOK
BELONGS TO:

_____

Birth date:

_____

Birth time:

_____

Birth location:

_____

ZODIAC SIGNS

TAURUS

ZODIAC SIGNS
TAURUS

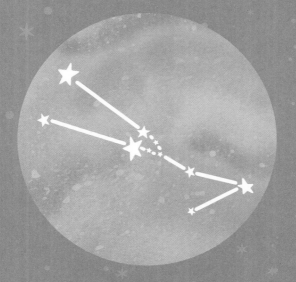

COURTNEY O'REILLY

STERLING ETHOS
New York

STERLING ETHOS
New York

An Imprint of Sterling Publishing Co., Inc.
1166 Avenue of the Americas
New York, NY 10036

ISBN 978-1-4549-3899-6

Library of Congress Cataloging-in-Publication Data

Names: O'Reilly, Courtney, author.
Title: Zodiac signs : Taurus : a sign-by-sign guide / Courtney O'Reilly.
Other titles: Taurus
Description: New York, New York : Sterling Publishing Co., Inc., 2020. |
   Includes bibliographical references and index. | Summary: "Illustrated
   authoritative guide for adults to the astrological sign of Taurus,
   including information about love life, work, school, family, and daily
   life"-- Provided by publisher.
Identifiers: LCCN 2019030314 | ISBN 9781454938996 (hardcover) |
   ISBN 9781454939115 (ebook)
Subjects: LCSH: Taurus (Astrology)
Classification: LCC BF1727.2 .O74 2020 | DDC 133.5/263--dc23
LC record available at https://lccn.loc.gov/2019030314

Distributed in Canada by Sterling Publishing Co., Inc.
c/o Canadian Manda Group, 664 Annette Street
Toronto, Ontario M6S 2C8, Canada
Distributed in the United Kingdom by GMC Distribution Services
Castle Place, 166 High Street, Lewes, East Sussex BN7 1XU, England
Distributed in Australia by NewSouth Books
University of New South Wales, Sydney, NSW 2052, Australia

For information about custom editions, special sales, and premium
and corporate purchases, please contact Sterling Special Sales at
800-805-5489 or specialsales@sterlingpublishing.com.

Manufactured in China

2 4 6 8 10 9 7 5 3 1

sterlingpublishing.com

Cover design by Elizabeth Mihaltse Lindy
Cover and endpaper illustration by Sarah Frances
Interior design by Nancy Singer
Zodiac signs ©wikki33 and macrovector/freepik

To my family, with love.

CONTENTS

INTRODUCTION

"If you always do what interests you, at least one person is pleased."

—KATHARINE HEPBURN, ACTOR AND
TAURUS SUN, BORN MAY 12

What an honor and thrill that you picked up this book and decided to read it; thank you from the bottom of my heart. This is my first book, and I suppose that as an astrologer I shouldn't be surprised by the timing, but I am nonetheless. At the time I signed on to write a book on Taurus for this series, the planet that rules astrology, surprises, and exciting out-of-the-blue change, Uranus, was on top of my natal sun in Taurus to the exact degree. I am thrilled to be a part of this wonderful series on the zodiac. Throughout this book I break down key components of what makes Taureans tick in all the different areas of their lives—childhood through adulthood, in love, at work, and in the world at large—in an easy-to-understand way with lots of examples. If you are a Taurus, I hope this serves as a helpful guide on your path to shine your very brightest. If you are reading to gain a better understanding of a particular Taurus in your life—perhaps a lover, dear friend, or boss—I hope it sheds light on your questions and offers greater insight. My highest goal with this book is to help you understand yourself and those around you a bit better with the hope of increasing compassion for both yourself and others through the lens of astrology.

Astrology is the study of possibility, not to be confused with predestination or religion. It is the study of planetary cycles—their placement at our birth and their continual motion thereafter, known by astrologers as transits—that affect our lives in ways both large and small. It is an invaluable tool used to explore our innate nature and understand those who orbit us in a more intimate and integrated way. For this reason, astrology is also a study in compassion, for once you see the scope of what an individual is working with, it's almost impossible not to feel compassion for that individual's situation—astrology is broadening and enlightening in this way. Astrology reveals the climate and condition, which we then can use to make more conscious decisions on how to make the most of what is in order to thrive and live the best life possible. We have free will, and you are the captain of your ship at all times. Astrology simply reveals potential we may have otherwise missed. It helps us maximize and make the most of our gifts and work with more intention and clarity through the challenges that surely will come.

Astrology has deep roots dating back to ancient times, with the people of Babylonia (present-day Iraq), Central America, India, Egypt, Greece, and China all developing their own methods. Those methods later mixed and blended, evolving over many years into astrology as we know it today. In his *Handbook for the Humanistic Astrologer*, Dane Rudhyar said, "Astrology is a language. If you understand this language, The Sky Speaks to You." It really does feel like translating another language at times—astrology is a rich and wonderful mix of ancient study infused with mythology and rooted in math and symbology.

We as individuals are a reflection of the cosmos at the moment we are born through what astrologers call a natal chart, or natal horoscope. We each carry within us the imprint of the luminaries: sun and moon, as well as all eight planets and each sign of the zodiac, spread across the twelve houses, which show how we relate to specific areas of our life such as love, career, and parenthood. You may be interested to learn that among the eight planets, the inner planets—Mercury, Venus, and Mars—along with the sun and moon, relate most to our personality, and Jupiter and Saturn, the two planets considered to be in between the inner and outer planets, show major trends of the time. The outer planets (Uranus, Neptune, and Pluto) are related to generational trends, since those planets are much farther away and move far more slowly than do the inner planets. While astronomers now classify Pluto as a dwarf planet, many astrologers still consider Pluto a planet. We see how potent Pluto's affect is within the chart. The slower a planet moves the longer it stays in one sign and area of your chart, which leaves a lasting impression. Pluto's powerful affect has not altered, and so in relation to astrology you will notice Pluto is still referred to as a planet. There is a series of sacred texts called the Hermetic Corpus written by Hermes Trismegistus, which includes the Emerald Tablet. The Emerald Tablet details one of the defining concepts of astrology—"As above, so below"; or in other words what occurs above (sky) affects below (Earth). Similarly, our inner workings affect our outer world and vice versa. Astrologer and author Betty Lundsted brilliantly explains this concept of "as above, so below" in her book *Astrological Insights into Personality*: "In an ancient religious manuscript, the author discusses the concept that the entire zodiac represents a person. The macrocosm and the microcosm reflect each other. 'As above so below.' In order to realize the full potential of personality and creativity in a lifetime, all the signs should be integrated within the individual. This integration process will make us 'whole.'"

Let's explore a few fundamental foundational points as you dive into this book and the others in this series. The first is that we all have two charts: what's called a solar chart, which is based on your sun sign, and a natal chart, which is based on your precise birth information. You can (and should!) read the two books in this series for your sun and rising signs. When you read horoscopes, you may want to read for the sun and rising signs as well. This will offer you a wider scope of understanding of yourself and current planetary happenings. Your solar chart is based on where the sun was when you were born and is what nearly every person you encounter will know about astrology: "What sign are you?" "Taurus!"

Your solar chart is an extremely important part of your personal astrology and nature, just as the sun is the center of our solar system. In the same way, it is the core within you. It illuminates the center of your essence—how you shine in the world, your vitality, and your ego identity—and offers great insight into your purpose and what you will enjoy and thrive at doing. This is why horoscopes are written for your sun sign—there is a reason all the other planets in our solar system dance around the sun and not the other way around. It is our brightest light and the life-sustaining source of energy for our planet.

If you were born between April 20 and May 20, you are a Taurus. If you were born very close to either the beginning or the end date listed, it's of critical importance that you find your exact time of birth to calculate whether the sun was in Aries or Taurus if you were born at the beginning of the season (April 20), or in Taurus or Gemini if you were born at the end (May 20). The sun changes sign at slightly different times each year, so if you were born on April 20 or May 20, there is a chance you are not a Taurus at all. You may have heard others refer to being on the "cusp"; what this really means is that you're born on the day the sun changes from one sign to the next. However, the sun cannot be in two places at once, so you're either one or the other. You must find your exact birth time to reveal the sun's precise placement at the moment of your birth. Locate your birth certificate, ask a parent or trusted relative who would remember, or alternatively, if you were born in the United States, you can contact the Bureau of Vital Statistics in the capital of the state in which you were born to purchase the long-form copy of your birth certificate, which includes birth time if it was recorded. Once you have the time, there are several resources online to calculate your natal chart for free. To calculate your natal chart, you will need your birth date, including the year; your exact time of birth; and your birth location. This chart will not only confirm your sun's placement but also determine what sign you have rising, or the sign that was coming up on Earth's eastern horizon when you were born. Your rising sign sets the layout of your completely individual natal chart. Your natal chart is unique to you and you alone—no two will be exactly the same.

Perhaps you've asked yourself, "How can it be that astrology divides all of humanity into twelve signs? Surely we are more individual than that." It's true! We each have the sun, the moon, and all eight planets manifesting their energetic pull within our lives. To further understand the complexities of your natal chart as it pertains to all of your planetary placements, seek out a skilled astrologer for a one-on-one consultation. In this book, though, we will be focusing on Taurus as a sun sign. If Taurus is your rising sign, this book is equally important for you, and I invite you to read it for a more rounded understanding of your deepest, truest nature.

Astrologers study the planets' movements through the twelve constellations the ancients deemed most impactful for us here on Earth. We are interested in the planetary conditions under which an individual was born, because depending on these conditions, some planets will be particularly impactful for that person. Each of the twelve signs has a planetary ruler, with Venus overseeing both Taurus and Libra. Yes, it's no surprise that sweet, sensual, earthy Taurus is Venus's child.

In Latin, Taurus means "The Bull": symbolically Taurus is represented by a circle (spirit) with a crescent moon on top (soul) that looks like the bull's horns. Taurus is strongly linked to agriculture and represents the time of year when the Earth is fertile and lush. We can also look to the mythology of Venus (Roman) and Aphrodite (Greek) for greater understanding of Taurus's motivations. Across cultures, Venus is considered the goddess of love and affection, receptivity, beauty, and friendship. Venus oversees all social interaction; anything she touches is softened and has an angelic glow. Venus imparts joy and fun! With Venus's guidance, a Taurus is good-humored with a magnetic allure that is hard to deny and a tactile style of affection that is simply irresistible.

Astrology is complex, but fortunately it offers us a few subsections to help explain the nuance and variation from sign to sign. These are known as the elements, modalities, and houses, with all the signs evenly divided within each subsection. We have four elements: fire (Aries, Leo, Sagittarius), earth (Taurus, Virgo, Capricorn), air (Gemini, Libra, Aquarius), and water (Cancer, Scorpio, Pisces), also known as triplicities, with three signs falling under each element. There are three modalities: cardinal (Aries, Cancer, Libra, Capricorn), fixed (Taurus, Leo, Scorpio, Aquarius), and mutable (Gemini, Virgo, Sagittarius, Pisces), also known as quadruplicities, with four signs under each modality. Finally there are twelve houses, with each sign traditionally claiming ownership of one house. The elements add texture to the quality of each sign; the modalities correlate with nature and align with the seasons; and the houses, which the twelve signs of the zodiac fall within, emphasize the different areas of our lives. Your natal chart reveals the layout of the zodiac around the twelve houses and thus shows which sign you have rising or which sign was on Earth's eastern horizon when you were born, as well as where the sun, the moon, and all eight planets fall within each of your natal horoscope's twelve houses.

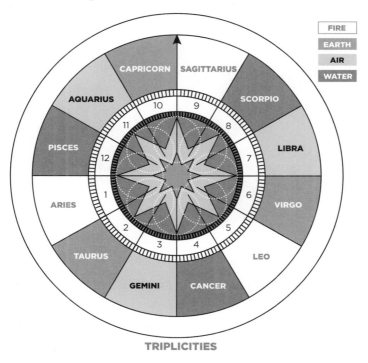

TRIPLICITIES

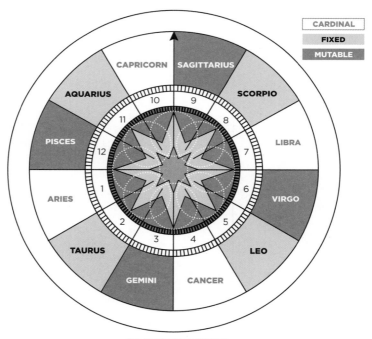

CARDINAL
FIXED
MUTABLE

CAPRICORN SAGITTARIUS
AQUARIUS SCORPIO
PISCES LIBRA
ARIES VIRGO
TAURUS LEO
GEMINI CANCER

QUADRUPLICITIES

Taurus is the fixed-earth sign of the zodiac, and like all the fixed signs, Taurus sustains the midpart of its season, which is spring, with Aries (cardinal) initiating the season and Gemini (mutable) ending the season. You can look to nature for information on every sign. Consider spring for a moment: Mother Nature is in full bloom, flowers greet us in abundance, trees are full with foliage that seems to have come to life overnight, as if they had not been bare just days before. There is a general lightness and a welcome warmth in the air. It's not the beginning (Aries; cardinal) or end (Gemini; mutable) of the spring—it's smack-dab in the middle (fixed). Taurus sustains all that's been initiated before releasing into the end of the season. In the same way, if you are a Taurus or have Taurus rising, you carry the sustaining qualities of a perpetual spring within you. Just as nature can't be rushed and steadily builds to bloom right on time, so it is with a Taurus.

Traditionally, the second of the twelve houses is Taurus's natural domain, with a focus on values, possessions, money, and self-esteem. This area of the chart offers insight into what we value most. We can learn much about our own self-esteem from the second house in both our solar and natal charts. It also offers insight into how we relate to material possessions and how we manage and leverage the resources available to us. Remember, Taurus is an earth sign, and so Taureans live in the practical realities of this world and are deeply enmeshed in pinpointing the task at hand and building it into a tangible reality. For this reason, the second house also correlates to ways in which we may earn monetary income. After all, money is a tangible resource, as any decent Taurus will gladly remind you.

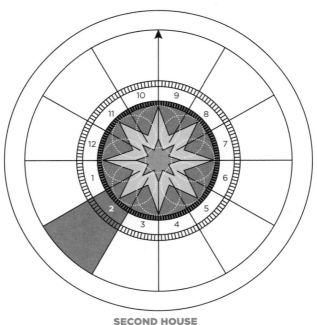

SECOND HOUSE

Remember, if you are a Taurus or have Taurus rising, you are a child of Venus, and so you are affected by her movements more than are the other signs, save for Libra, as Venus rules both Taurus and Libra. For this reason, pay close attention to when your favorite astrologer discusses Venus changing from one sign into another, which happens about every three and half weeks, especially when Venus retrogrades, which is once every eighteen months, to last approximately six weeks. Mark these dates on your calendar, as they will be periods in which you're especially sensitive to the energetic shifts at play. With Venus retrograde, you'll want to note that it is not a good time to launch a business or something you hope to be financially fruitful or for anything beauty related (think cosmetic surgery or drastic changes to your appearance).

Now that we've covered those fundamentals, I truly hope you enjoy your time spent exploring the chapters that follow. May this book spark joy, produce "aha" moments, and assist you in solidifying your understanding of the zodiac's most down-to-earth sign, Taurus.

TAURUS

as a Child

"Dreams can become a reality when we possess a vision that is characterized by the willingness to work hard, a desire for excellence, and a belief in our right and our responsibility to be equal members of society."

—JANET JACKSON, SINGER, SONGWRITER, DANCER, ACTOR, AND TAURUS SUN, BORN MAY 16

To explore a child's experience of their unique astrological makeup requires a different approach than one used in exploring the chart of an adult, whose life is much farther along in the layers of its unfolding. Children's charts offer exciting insight into the seeds of their potential; their character is considered malleable and not yet fully formed. Children are still in the beginning stages of their lives, and thus everything related to a child's chart is an opportunity to root into. As a parent, investing in understanding your child's astrology will offer a wealth of knowledge about how to best guide and develop your child's innate gifts and skills and also will provide helpful information on navigating areas in life that may be a little tougher for your wee Taurus. The idea is to nurture and guide your child toward activities, teachers, and resources that may help them grow into their unique potentials and flourish on their path. Astrology can be such a helpful resource for parents! In this section you will learn more about what it means to have your little one's brightest light, their sun, in the sign of Taurus.

The child whose sun or rising sign is in Taurus is sensitive to their surroundings, as Taurus is the most sensual and sensory-oriented sign of the zodiac. These are the children who while playing outside will stop along the way to literally smell the roses, run their tiny fingers along a brick wall as they find the texture exhilarating, or sing along and dance with musicians and performers on the street. They are completely enthralled with worldly delights and have an uncanny knack for effortlessly finding them wherever they go. They also may be more attached to physical items as a source of comfort than are children of other signs: a blanket, a stuffed animal, or the tactile comfort of sucking one's thumb. I myself am a Taurus and admit I sucked my thumb until I was seven. It was an impossible habit to break. I found a deep sense of comfort in sucking my thumb or gently running my finger along my eyelid or the top part of my ear to fall asleep. Something about the texture and connection to habit itself was soothing. I also had a small purple blanket sprinkled with tiny sparkly silver stars (the foreshadowing!) named Blankie that I would take everywhere. I couldn't leave the house without it, and if I couldn't find it, I would be completely distraught until it was located. To say I was attached is to put it lightly. I was so in love with Blankie that I refused to allow my aunt and grandmother to make me a new one despite their pleading. I loved on Blankie so hard for so long that by the end it was in tatters. Even after I no longer needed Blankie, I didn't have the heart to toss it and so held on to it in a little box for years; its remains were mostly polyester stuffing with a few scraps of ratty purple fabric dotted with long-since-faded stars that I literally tied back together in knots as pieces fell off. I share this to show how deep Taureans' attachment can run to an item or habit we hold close to heart.

The planet Venus is Taurus's guiding light, and that imbues these children's nature with tenderness. Taurean children tend to be quite charming. They are warm and affectionate, bestowing you with an abundance of hugs, kisses, cuddles, and "I love yous"—they are sweet as can be, a true joy, and overall their temperament is easygoing. However, when they get upset, they're likely to be physical, using tough little fists and feet in protest, and probably forceful too—Taureans tend to have a sturdy build and a naturally strong constitution.

In the body, Taurus rules the neck, throat, vocal cords, and ears, and that gives these children a natural attunement to music, particularly singing and the performance arts in general. They are the children most likely to be your back-seat entertainment (aside from Leo, of course), loving to sing along in the car, belting their tiny lungs out to today's greatest hits, not missing a beat and surprisingly on key. They also enjoy being sung to, so be sure to join in. Taurus is an exceedingly creative sign—there is a love and appreciation of art, dance, and music.

Thrilled by worldly delights and generally relaxed, they have an affable nature that ensures that they naturally make friends wherever they go. Their inclination toward physicality means a good run around the playground or a soothing drive in the car will have them out like a light, fully surrendering to naptime, in no time. This is not to say that they don't have a stubborn streak, which they surely do as one of the four fixed signs of the zodiac, the others being Leo, Aquarius, and Scorpio. Natives of the fixed signs are built to sustain, and so once they've made up their minds, redirecting them may prove to be a true challenge. Taurus children who have set their sights on something and have been told no are likely to dig in their heels and raise their fists in solid protest. Their will is so strong that they're likely to tire you out with their steadfastness rather than the other way around. Explain in practical terms what you're asking rather than making blunt demands—they'll eventually come around when they feel it was their own decision to do so. They have a strong will and attach to material things and loved ones deeply. Because of this, a kind of possessiveness may pervade them; as a young person, their sense of security is still forming, and so a parent or teacher requesting they share their most prized toy with someone else may throw them for a loop. However, Taurus children are typically generous as long as it's understood that the precious possession in question belongs to them at the end of the day.

Taurus children are delighted when it comes to mealtime, and they love to go out to eat—the whole experience feels like an exotic thrill. From real flowers on the table and the feel of the tablecloth to deciding what to order, they love the sense of community gathering around the table to share something delicious has the power to create. There is deep comfort to be found in a shared meal with people you love; it's one of life's simplest and most profound gifts. Food unites, nourishes, and comforts. A friend whose younger brother is a Taurus shared that when the siblings were young, the brother would randomly shout "Apple pie!" He'd wake up and gleefully announce "Apple pie!" or walk into a room and declare "Apple pie!"—it became a kind of official proclamation on the celebration of food and the joy of dessert within their family. His love of food, and clearly apple pie, was loud and clear from a young age.

Taurean children are tactile learners. They do well with immersive experiences to accompany their book learning and school assignments. This will help solidify their understanding through being able to get their hands dirty, build, touch, and fully experience the information introduced with all their senses. For this reason, they're sure to love recess and field trips. Recess offers a chance to get outside and experience the glory of nature, and school field trips to the aquarium, the museum, and historic sites offer the chance to learn in the hands-on way they really thrive with and adore.

On a similar note, teaching them early on the value of their effort, time, and resources through helping out around the house with chores is great for young Taureans. If they seem a little bored or are leaning toward laziness, give them a task! They'll perk right up at the chance to do something to be helpful—they relish the experience of seeing a project through and flourish on the appreciation that comes with a job well done. Offer an allowance for their effort, even if it's small. Since this is one of the signs most naturally inclined toward finances and managing resources, starting them off with a strong foundation around earning and saving will set them up for success and fine-tune their natural ability to accumulate wealth and manage their financial security later in life.

Taurus children do well with routines that are stuck to. They're not big fans of change, so introducing a change too quickly would likely have you in a standoff with a small person that may very well outlast you—Taurus kids can hold firm till the cows come home! They crave the comfort of what is known and familiar—they are creatures of habit. They find their routines soothing and steadying, which is important to them, as this is a security-oriented sign. Change is a necessary part of life, but when introducing it to a young Taurus, you will have more pleasant results for all parties involved if you do so slowly and over time whenever possible. Remain solid and consistent yourself, showing by example that all is well and that change is completely natural and nothing to fret about. Speaking of habits, ensure that good ones are set in place and try to nip any poor habits right away, as these little ones latch on to consistent habits quickly and it will be arduous to break a bad habit once they become accustomed to it.

As a Taurus child, I loved to put on little shows for my baby brother. I would set up the living room as my personal stage and dance around and maybe share a little impromptu song I was making up in the moment. Actually, as far back as

I can remember, I have always loved to dance and sing, and singing in the car was my favorite! As a child I was obsessed with Whitney Houston—I knew every word of every song she sang. Her voice is perfection, and my Taurean sensibilities have always known it. You may be surprised by your little Taurus's natural sense of pitch at a young age. My friends and I were constantly putting together dance routines and loved competing in the lip-sync battle as part of our homecoming festivities in high school. My two besties, another Taurus and a Gemini, took it very seriously, putting together elaborate choreography and costumes and rehearsing to perfection for months in advance, every detail in place. We placed in the top three every year, with our senior year an all-out extravaganza to Michael Jackson's "Thriller," complete with a dozen other classmates as zombies popping out of seats in the audience. We were good too, so good that we had teachers trying to get us to spill what we'd do leading up to each year's competition, with other classmates spying on us to see what we had planned. Years later on a visit home, I ran into the band teacher at a coffee shop, and he told me that after we graduated the lip-sync competition was never the same. This is one of a Taurus's greatest skills: combining their talents with their above-average diligence to achieve a level of excellence through consistent effort, which inspires others around them to do the same.

TAURUS

as an Adult

"You have got to discover you, what you do, and trust it."

—Barbra Streisand, singer, actor, filmmaker, and Taurus Sun, born April 24

The Taurus Sun or Taurus rising person has a soothing, steady presence. These individuals radiate a natural sense of calm wherever they go. When they are with you, they give you their full attention. Making those around them feel seen and heard is a rare gift of theirs. They are the friends of the zodiac who will gently touch your arm rather than speak to make their presence known, are generous with hugs at both hello and good-bye, and hold your hand tight when sharing an emotional story. You can trust your steadfast, devoted Taurus friend to be there to comfort you when you need it. Not only will Taurus friends be there, they will arrive with wine in hand, a perfectly paired cheese to match, and a willing ear ready to listen. Their attention is fully focused; they are great listeners and do not rush you— you will have their undivided attention. Their patience is admirable and is part of what makes them so likable. They exude grace and charm and have an easygoing way about them, and they tend to get along with most people. They are sure to make you laugh and feel loved, all with a little twinkle in their eyes; they enjoy spreading joy. They have a warm glow about them, thanks to Venus, the planet of love, affection, and friendship that governs their sign.

Taureans are patient and persistent; they take their time to make a decision, but when they do, they make it with their whole will and heart. You can count on them to follow through on what they've said they will do. Exploring the world with a Taurus is a luxurious experience, as this is the most sensory-oriented sign of the zodiac. Each of their senses is heightened, and that gives them refined tastes. Want to experience the best the world has to offer? Befriend a Taurus, and they will lead the way. They'll take you to the best new restaurant in the neighborhood, a gorgeous part of the park you hadn't noticed before, or an exceptional music venue featuring unparalleled talent—their taste is impeccable. Their finely tuned senses won't allow them to settle for less, and so they won't let you, their dear friend, colleague, or lover, settle for less either!

They are also some of the most reliable people you will ever meet. If they commit themselves to a task, you can bet your bottom dollar they will follow through. They are thorough too; they may be slow moving, but trust that what needs doing will be done with the utmost care and attention. Taureans have a strong sense of their own values. They are rock solid, and that is one of the greatest benefits of knowing and loving them. This quality can be frustrating at times, however. I say this because Taureans are so steadfast, they can end up a bit stuck in their ways. They are the fixed-earth sign of the zodiac, after all. I like to say, "A Taurus in motion stays in motion." This means that once they are set on their course, they are unlikely to change because you have told them to or have suggested another way of doing things. Taureans much prefer to deal with change on their own terms and in their own time. Just like the bull, they are slow and steady and unmovable until they decide it's time to move. Offer your insight, then give them time and space. They will come around once they have had time to consider all the options and realize you have a good point. They are security-oriented creatures, so change is no thrill for them. They much prefer the known tried-and-true way of doing things. Why rock the boat? Why fix what isn't broken? They have a reputation for clinging to habits, and so veering from the known is unsettling to them. However, their steadfastness is what makes them such loyal lifelong comrades, and they will prove time and again to be a stable anchor through some of life's most rocky moments. They aren't the ones who flee when the going gets tough. This is not to say that Taureans don't have limits—they do. They just have a wide threshold, as they're very tolerant. Still, a Taurus pushed too far is no joke. It takes a lot to rile them, as the bull is stable and unmovable, but when they are provoked too hard, you can have quite the fury on your hands.

Taureans are sensual souls, using all their senses to navigate the world around them. They make spectacular lovers for this reason. There is a transcendence in their touch, a tranquility innate within their voice, and a radiant warmth to their aura. Because they are ruled by the planet Venus, their affections are infused with a level of grace and warmth completely individual to their sign. There will be no doubt you're cared for when you date a Taurus. They'll wine you, dine you . . . and, well, you get the picture! When they care for you, they invest in you through the selfless offering of their time, energy, and resources. They're true-blue loyal to the ones they love and thrive on appreciation in return for their efforts. Taurus is a receptive sign: Taureans give love openly but also need this kind of openness in return. They tend to stay present in the current moment rather than dwelling on the past or fretting about the future—as their heightened senses keep them connected to what's happening in the moment.

Taurus is all about values with a capital V. They carefully and thoughtfully select their things, think big purchases through, and take pride in their wardrobe of hand-selected prized pieces made of the finest fabrics in beautiful shades. To give a personal example, when I traveled to Greece, there was a miscommunication concerning my luggage. I was headed to Crete but first had a layover in Athens, and the attendant checking my bag heard only Athens. When I arrived in Crete, I watched as hundreds of bags were carousselled out. Being the good little Taurus I am, I waited patiently as the crowd eventually thinned until there were only two of us remaining, with no more bags. After about an hour of waiting, the panic set in. Oh, no! My precious, carefully curated things! As I filled out the claim to find my bag in Athens and have it sent to Crete, I did mental gymnastics, thinking of my favorite pieces—some of them irreplaceable should my bag not be found. This cataloging of possessions is a classic tactic I subconsciously revert to as a means of protecting myself, to make sure I am safe— because as you now know, we Taureans are a fixed sign, and we hold tightly to our perceptions of security. We like to stick to what we know works. When a wrench gets thrown into the mix, it can make our whole system go haywire. My travel buddy, whose sun and rising signs are mutable, or flexible, signs, was cool as a cucumber, saying this had happened to her twice and both times the bag was recovered, no problem. Once, she told me, it even happened hours before she had an appearance on television! I was horrified at the thought, though she was able to laugh about it and seemed unconcerned. This is an excellent example of why we need an eclectic mix of people of all signs in our lives. Her flexibility in the moment was enough to shake me loose from my tight fixed grip on the situation and make me consider a different way of reacting. They found my bag and returned it to me the very next day. Crisis averted. I share this story to show how we Taureans are so attached to the physical. Our sensitive sensory system makes us more attuned to the tangible world around us, and so we attach meaning to and place special emphasis on our prized possessions. Oh, and by the way, one such prized possession in my bag that day was a one-of-a-kind vintage silk blouse, the most delicate pink with a hand-painted rose on it—can you get any more Venusian than that?

In their careers, Taureans take a pragmatic approach. As security-oriented beings, they like to know what's expected of them, and of course, being ruled by Venus, they are focused on finances. Figuring out how to grow their nest egg is important to them, as well as feeling valued for their time and efforts. Venus rules love and relationships. It is considered what's known as a "benefic planet," as whatever Venus touches tends to have a beneficial outcome, including aspects of our lives related to money. With Venus as their planetary ruler, Taureans have a leg up when it comes to financial savvy. As one of my beloved mentors, Susan Miller, likes to say, "Taurus is the sign most likely to be at home on a Friday night with nice glass of wine, reviewing their bank statement." They are naturally skilled and practical when it comes to taking an idea, shaping it into something tangible that can turn a profit, and then making that profit multiply through diligent planning, saving, and investing. They are particularly adept when it comes to finances and managing resources to maximize results. Taurus traditionally oversees the second house, the area of the chart related to earned income, and so with wise decision making, Taureans are likely to accumulate wealth throughout their lifetimes.

Venus's influence assists Taureans in finding success in a number of fields, such as the performing arts, dance, and especially singing; they are often gifted vocally, with many well-known singers being Taureans. They also do well in professions that entail managing money, tending to the land, or working with food, such as banking, financial planning, real estate, farming, and landscaping, or in the culinary arts as a chef or sommelier. They may have great success in trades that involve caring for our physical form, including bodywork such as massage and in beauty-related professions such as a perfumer.

TAURUS

as a Parent

"If the day ever came when we were able to accept ourselves and our children exactly as we and they are, then, I believe, we would have come very close to an ultimate understanding of what 'good' parenting means."

—FRED ROGERS, TELEVISION PERSONALITY, MUSICIAN, PUPPETEER, WRITER, PRODUCER, MINISTER, AND TAURUS RISING WITH SUN IN PISCES, BORN MARCH 20

What we discussed in the chapter on Taurus children is equally relevant and important to remember here; a child's unique astrological makeup cannot be approached in the same way you would explore an adult's astrology. An adult has lived a life that is layered and complex. Whereas children are at the precipice of their life, they're just beginning to dive in, and everything related to their personal astrology represents an opportunity waiting to be developed. If you are a parent, you are the lucky one who gets to decide how to help your children navigate their astrology, to offer them the guidance and opportunities that help them not only trust their gifts but hone them as well.

As a parent, your chart and your child's chart are intrinsically linked, as the child's natal chart is the planetary weather, known as transits, you were experiencing on the day your child was born! For this reason, your charts, when layered together, give great insight into the way you relate to each other and can provide helpful clues to how to nurture with clear intention on the basis of the child's individual needs displayed within their chart. Because each of our charts is completely unique, it makes sense to honor the needs of each individual's chart. Your child may have interests and needs very different from your own, and their chart can offer helpful clues to what these are and lessen confusion or resentment if later in life your child chooses a direction in life much different from yours.

Home and family are matters of deep importance to Taureans. They take great care in creating a well-thought-out plan for success that includes how they will earn, save, invest, and create a safe and secure home space for themselves and their loved ones. This is one of their greatest gifts to their families: their reliability and endurance come what may. They will strive consistently to find a solution to maintain a sense of security for their families as best they can. The same principles apply when they are parenting. They are present and engaged, and their kids benefit from their focused attention, lots of hands-on teaching, and plenty of affection.

A Taurus parent doesn't shy away from offering up an abundance of loving words and physical attention: affirming pats, hugs, kisses, and cuddles. They are good-humored parents and enjoy creating characters for bedtime stories or playing make-believe and dressing up with their kiddos—in fact they quite enjoy it, as it gives them an opportunity to use their talents through voice and physical play. Creative activities are some of the best outlets for Taurus parents to connect with their children, as creative play comes naturally to them, and they may find that their kids' sense of wonder reinvigorates their own.

Nature is another prime outlet for the Taurus parent, as the sign rules the center of spring. A Taurus client once shared that when she thinks of her childhood, she's immediately taken back to memories of her grandparents' house in the woods. Long walks through the trees, trying to swing on a weeping willow, spotting a deer sipping from a pond, picking strawberries, jumping into a pile of freshly raked leaves, letting pets run free in the yard, looking at colorful flowers, helping in the garden, and having picnics are some of her most vivid and fond memories. She looks forward to creating similiar memories with her own kids one day. Taurus parents pass on love, appreciation, and respect for nature and all its beauty to their children.

Given the innate steadfast nature of Taureans, they

swear by the power of habit, incorporating solid bed and wake-up times, mealtimes, and homework rituals. Consistency over time comforts them, and so it makes sense to them to pass the ethos of this cherished trait on to their children as if to say, "I'm here, I'm not going anywhere, you can count on me." They make solid parents, because they pride themselves on sticking to what they've started. They also say what they mean and mean what they say. They take their time to come to a conclusion, as they want to be sure they can really stand by what they say before they say it. This is helpful to their kids because it offers clarity around the ground rules. They are patient parents as well and don't mind having to repeat the same concept over and over until it settles in and to review and repeat rules and lessons until their child fully absorbs the teaching at hand. They understand that some things just can't be rushed.

Because this is the fixed-earth sign of the zodiac, Taureans are down to earth, literally—they love to get outside and walk barefoot through the grass, to roll around, throw a ball, or build a sand castle. They are hands-on parents, present in the moment and full of affection. Taurus is one of the most nurturing signs as a result of Venus's warm influence and its ruling element, earth. It is no different with Taureans' children—they will be fed and cared for. Taurus parents will strive to maximize the means and resources available to them in order to take the very best possible care of their babies.

They also take joy in passing on their refined sense of taste and love of the arts. Whenever possible, they will try to enrich their children's lives by offering experiences with and insight into the arts. Trips to the museum, a ballet, a Broadway show, or even a specialty grocery store or a local farm with a petting zoo where they can learn about nature and agriculture are memories the child of a Taurean parent is sure to cherish.

Taurus natives adore good food—all aspects of it really. They care about where it came from, the quality, and its textures, consistency, color, and smell. From growing to cooking to eating, they attach great meaning to food and love the power food has to bring people together. For all these reasons it's no surprise that Taureans are a wiz in the kitchen. Bringing their kids into the kitchen, whether it's to put together a simple snack, whip up a batch of chocolate chip cookies for the school bake sale, or include them in regular dinner prep each night, makes for a fun bonding experience between Taurus parents and their kids. They may be easier to cajole into extra dessert requests than other parents as well, since they themselves are an easy sell on an extra serving. The truth is that they want to indulge too! It's fair to say that Taurus parents can lean toward being indulgent. However, they are just as likely to encourage getting outside for fresh air and some exercise, so generally speaking there is a balance.

Taurus parents instill in their children a sense of awareness, respect, and appreciation for ownership of their possessions, as well as an admiration for the land, and for this reason their children are likely to be respectful of others' possessions and values outside of their own. They understand the work involved and the time it takes to accumulate and build something you love, thanks to their parent's unwavering example.

TAURUS

in Love

"I was born with an enormous need for affection, and a terrible need to give it."

—AUDREY HEPBURN, ACTOR, HUMANITARIAN, FASHION ICON, AND TAURUS SUN, BORN MAY 4

T aurus is ruled by the planet of love and affection, Venus. Under Venus's tutelage, a Taurus native has a magnetic allure that is impossible to deny and a tactile style of affection that is simply irresistible, not to mention that Taureans are overall easygoing with a great sense of humor. Taureans are some of the most affectionate and receptive people with whom you could hope to pair. Their delicate sensory abilities steer them straight toward the finest wine, first-rate restaurants, fine chocolates, soft floral perfumes, and dreamy lush locales for vacationing. You are lucky if you love a Taurus, as you'll reap the benefits of accompanying them on their elevated sensory adventures.

In the introduction to this book, we discussed how each of the signs has an element and modality with which it correlates. Since Taurus is the fixed-earth sign, Taureans find common ground and harmony with other earth signs, which are Virgo and Capricorn, and also with the water signs: Cancer, Scorpio, and Pisces. If you consider the elements and the ways they may blend, it's easy to see that earth and water are a natural duo, with earth absorbing water and the combination creating the perfect climate for abundant growth. Taureans may feel a strong bond with the other fixed signs as well, as there is a sense of kinship in their abilities to sustain and see something through. Fellow fixed signs are Leo (fixed-fire), Scorpio (fixed-water), and Aquarius (fixed-air). I should also mention that there is potential for some butting of heads with the fixed combos, as each stands firm in its own right.

TAUREANS' COMPATIBILITY WITH THE OTHER SIGNS OF THE ZODIAC

I am asked all the time, "Are there signs I should avoid or signs I shouldn't be with?" I believe any two signs can work together romantically or otherwise with a little love and effort. Every relationship offers us an opportunity to grow, and so I would never recommend dismissing people because of their signs. Please don't do that, because you will close yourself off to such a wide pool of experience and potentially wonderful connection if you do. Each of the signs is equally valid and has its own wonders, gifts, and complexities to uncover and learn from. Don't limit yourself!

This is of course in reference to an individual's sun sign, so also keep in mind that you each have several other factors to consider as they relate to the complexities of your charts as a whole. The combinations with Taurus below can be interpreted from a romantic perspective, though the descriptions can easily apply to friendship and business relationships as well. Just adjust the wording to suit your situation for helpful clues to how Taurus works together with each of the other signs. Now, let's take a look and see how Taurus plays with the rest of the zodiac.

Taurus with Aries (cardinal-fire)

These two are quite different: Aries thrives on initiation, action, and loves to go, go, go, whereas Taureans much prefer to take their time and work slowly toward a goal. Perhaps you will butt heads on this from time to time, but Aries reminds their Taurus companion to take change in stride and get out of their comfort zone, and Taurus has an anchoring effect for Aries.

Taurus with Taurus (fixed-earth)

A pair of Taureans are right at home together. You're on the same page; you just get each other. You have the same Venusian sensibilities and share a love of the arts, music, delicious food, and life's comforts. This is a double dose of fixed-earth, however, which means it may be easy to fall into the same old patterns and routines together. You'll have to intentionally find ways to spice it up from time to time to keep things fresh!

Taurus with Gemini (mutable-air)

Geminis are mentally astute and quite clever, with varied interests. They tend to enjoy a detached way of living, which may prove a challenge for a Taurus. Taureans much prefer the comforts and security that a forever home, stable job, and attached relationship bring. The gift of this combo is that Gemini may teach Taurus the joys of letting go and wandering where one's curiosity leads, whereas Taurus shows Gemini the benefit of seeing an interest through and the joy of mastering a skill because of one's steadfastness.

Taurus with Cancer (cardinal-water)

This is a very sweet combo. Taurus and Cancer are both quite sensitive, and they both love the security of home, family time, cooking, and cuddling and are equally protective of what they've created together. Cancer is connected to matters of home and establishing a place that feels warm and loving, whereas Taurus works hard to create a sense of security that stabilizes and maintains that home life. You'll want an invitation to their dinner parties!

Taurus with Leo (fixed-fire)

Leo and Taurus really know how to have a good time. The two share an affinity for luxury, fine dining, and being an active part of the local cultural scene, not to mention that both are extremely creative in their own right. Their fixed natures create a mutual understanding, although from a different perspective, there is the potential for both parties to be quite headstrong when there's a disagreement. Taurus needs affection and appreciation, and Leo needs attention and respect. If both can learn to meet each other on those things, they'll be on their way.

Taurus with Virgo (mutable-earth)

Taurus and fellow earth sign Virgo get along beautifully, as they share a desire to build something of worth and integrity and are each naturally humble. Virgo is the mutable-earth sign, whereas Taurus is the fixed-earth sign. Virgo's flexibility helps Taurus see the value in pivoting when necessary so that things don't get too rigid, and Taurus's ability to follow through on promises made is reassuring to Virgo.

Taurus with Libra (cardinal-air)

Libra is a super-social sign and is most at home through connection to others. Social interactions stimulate their airy qualities assisting them to explore perspectives outside their own, which they enjoy. Taurus is not antisocial by any means but doesn't need the level of social stimulation Libra may want. Taureans like to sit with an idea, mull it over, and come to their own conclusion, whereas Libras like to get everyone's opinion to determine what makes the most sense based on varied perspectives. They do share Venus as their planetary ruler, and that creates harmony between them. They are truly a pair in their warmheartedness and softness and in their commitment to the ideals of beauty, grace, and pleasure.

Taurus with Scorpio (fixed-water)

This combo proves that opposites really do attract. Polarity is the word used to describe opposing signs, or signs that sit 180 degrees across the wheel from one another. Scorpio is the sign that sits opposite Taurus. It may sounds counterintuitive, but actually opposing signs have a natural affinity for each other—they tend to balance each other. Taurus and Scorpio are both fixed signs: Taurus is the fixed-earth sign, and Scorpio is the fixed-water sign. They each have a staunch attitude thanks to their fixed natures, and their elements—earth and water—create the ideal alchemy. Earth absorbs water, creating the perfect environment for life to grow and flourish. Both are determined and aren't easily steered off course, and that could potentially create competitiveness—though they tend to see eye to eye, but from opposing perspectives. Scorpios approach a situation by using their intuition and emotional intelligence as a result of their water influence, whereas Taureans take a more logical and grounded approach because of their earthy qualities.

Taurus with Sagittarius (mutable-fire)

Sagittarians are freedom loving and changeable, and their untethered nature can feel unsettling for a Taurus, whereas a Taurus's set ways and inflexibility can feel a bit too prohibitive for a Sagittarius. The two will need to be dedicated to understanding the other's perspective and compromise to accommodate the other's needs. The beauty of this combo, however, is that Sagittarius will inspire and ignite Taurus to action, and Taurus will offer Sagittarius practical advice that gives their big-picture dreams a firm footing.

Taurus with Capricorn (cardinal-earth)

Fellow earth sign Capricorn is a natural fit with Taurus. Taurus admires Capricorn's tenacity and hardworking nature. Their ability to set a goal with practical steps to achieve it is a real turn-on for Taurus, whereas Capricorn's sometimes doubtful nature appreciates Taurus's tender heart, honesty, and encouragement to stay the course. The two also have similar goals in regard to building their assets, bank accounts, and list of accolades for their hard work. There is mutual understanding with these two.

Taurus with Aquarius (fixed-air)

Aquarians have their sights set on the future. They're more interested in where we're going than in where we've been, whereas Taureans prefer to remain squarely in the present. Taurus may have a hard time understanding why Aquarius wants to re-create what's already been established, and Aquarius will be perplexed by Taurus's attachment to material things and immutable concepts of security, much preferring a detached mode of being. There will be challenges to meeting each other in the middle, though they are both fixed signs—Taurus is the fixed-earth, and Aquarius is fixed-air. There is respect for each other's commitment to a cause but sometimes conflicts in working together to achieve it.

Taurus with Pisces (mutable-water)

Taurus and Pisces make for a dreamy duo. Both are highly creative, and their earth and water combo is fertile ground for inspired artistic pursuits. There is a shared love for film, the theater, dance, and definitely music, and they'll never be at a loss for activities to do together. Pisces is more detached from earthly necessities than Taurus. Pisceans are not materialistic and don't care much for money or the mundane realities of life, whereas Taureans care deeply about the material world, and creating a sense of tangible security through their home and financial resources. Differences in this area may baffle both partners, but there are helpful connections within these differences. Pisces fluidity and flexibility remind Taurus of the importance of giving back and being charitable with their resources, as nothing is permanent, whereas Taurus's stable rootedness assists Pisces in making more of their inspired visions tangible realities than would be the case if they were on their own. There is a softness to each of these signs that ensures a tender, gentle, and loving combo.

TAURUS LOVER

When a Taurus loves you, you will know it; there will be no question about it. Their affection will be apparent in the kindness and tenderness of their words and touch; they can be quite sentimental and poetic as a result of their creative inclinations. As Taurean and queen of jazz Ella Fitzgerald said, "I guess what everyone wants more than anything else is to be loved. And to know that you loved me for my singing is too much for me. Forgive me if I don't have all the words. Maybe I can sing it and you'll understand." Their love is clear, honest, and genuine. There's not a lot of game playing or confusion (assuming there aren't any complicated aspects to their natal Venus or moon, for example). There is a kind admirable simplicity to a Taurus's affection—it's warm, sensual, and unwavering. It may take Taureans a while to decide you're the one for them, but don't take offense; this is because they are careful. They're not likely to rush into something or make rash decisions about the gift of their affection, but once they decide, they are all in. Taurus is one of the most devoted partners you could ever ask for and will stand by your side through and through. Loyalty is major for Taureans. Once they've decided you're the one for them, they become deeply invested and will do almost anything for you. To be clear, they expect the same kind of loyalty and commitment in return and don't handle a breach or lack of it well. They are loyal almost to a fault, at times staying the course when it would be best to leave. However, if a lack of loyalty is clear from the get-go, they're likely to back out as the connection just won't feel sustainable to them.

When you are dating a Taurus, consistency and follow-through really get their heart rate up. Ask them out and follow through, with no rescheduling multiple times, no flaky hard-to-get games; show them you're interested and then see the plan through. As this is an earth sign, their preference leans solidly toward in-person dating as opposed to long distance, since they crave the comfort of tactile experiences, especially with their love. It would be burdensome to not see or touch their beloved for long periods. They are well versed in body language, and no amount of video chat or texting could replace that for them. Taureans are sensualists; they enjoy physical affection, and that transfers to the bedroom as well—Taurus is inherently gifted in regard to sexual prowess. They aim to please and be pleased and are not shy with the gift of their attention; they enjoy doting on their lovers.

A fun first date for a Taurus may include going to an acclaimed restaurant with rave reviews, a walk in the park with fair-trade locally roasted coffee in hand, finding a cozy garden cafe to sip wine and lose yourselves in intimate conversation, or sharing your favorite art exhibit or museum with them. These experiences will make them feel seen and cherished and are a surefire way to impress them.

TAURUS PARTNER

When the time comes to take it to the next level with a Taurus, such as moving in together, you can be sure that the lease will be reviewed in full, mail will be forwarded ahead of time, the moving truck will be booked well in advance, and utilities will be scheduled to come on upon move-in. They are thorough people. Although they move at their own pace and cannot be rushed, you can trust that all will be accomplished as a result of their thought-out methodical approach. You'll enjoy an upgrade to your living space too thanks to your Taurus love's inclination toward all that is luxurious and comfort-oriented. Think soft lighting, lush fabrics, comfortable furnishings with beautiful natural finishes in hardwood, and lots of plants in an effort to invite nature indoors.

In dating and marriage alike, Taureans are loyal and true. Their close relationships are precious to them, and so they work hard to provide a stable and secure home life for themselves and their loved ones. They are present and attentive as well as supportive of a partner's goals. It really feels like a team effort when you're in it with a Taurus.

TAURUS
at Work

"I don't accept the status quo. I do accept Visa, MasterCard, or American Express."

—STEPHEN COLBERT, COMEDIAN, WRITER, PRODUCER, TELEVISION HOST, AND TAURUS SUN, BORN MAY 13

TAURUS

Taureans are hard workers; they sometimes get a bad rap for being lazy, but they actually love to be useful. They will be the ones to ensure that a project is seen all the way through, beginning to end, with all the boxes checked. They are thorough through and through and much prefer something done well over time to something done at half quality but completed quickly. As the sign that sustains the season of spring, they aren't concerned with rushing. As Lao Tzu said, "Nature does not hurry, yet everything is accomplished."

In the body, Taurus rules the throat, vocal cords, and thyroid as well as the ears. Taureans are sensitive to sound—as a sign ruled by Venus, they have a refined ear for music and often have quite skilled vocal abilities. They adore the arts and may be drawn to pursue them through careers as performers, dancers, artists, and vocalists. They may also have much success in beauty and healing services that incorporate the body, such as an esthetician or massage therapist. My lifelong best friend Cassandra, another Taurus, born the day after me, April 26, is a dancer and yoga teacher. Her yoga classes are very hands-on and almost always include essential oils on her warmed hands for students to inhale during the final Savasana, or final relaxation pose, and usually incorporate a little neck massage too, ensuring that her students release fully into a relaxed state. Her area of expertise is restorative yoga and Yoga Nidra, variations meant to slow one down and calm the nervous system. How Taurean is that? She once shared with me that she often finds it easier to express herself through dance, using her body rather than spoken words. It makes sense, doesn't it? With their heightened sensory abilities, it seems Taureans have easier access to expression through the body—touch, smell, taste, and sound—as opposed to words alone, which rely on logic, to get their message across.

On a similar note, one of the loveliest facials I've ever received was with an esthetician who had Taurus rising. It incorporated facial massage that was downright intuitive, and everything down to the dimmed lighting and music at precisely the correct subdued volume was just right—Taurus knows how to create an atmosphere. Their ruling planet, Venus, has much to do with their atmospheric discernment. Venus rules the sensual but doesn't stop there.

As I mentioned in Chapter 2, Venus also oversees finances, and so Taureans may very well be skilled in banking and finance positions as well as real estate. Their earthy nature means they may thrive in fields that deal with food, such as gourmet grocery and catering, as chefs or sommeliers, and in farming.

Venus also relates to women and women's causes, and the divine feminine nature within all of us (which we all have regardless of how we identify in terms of gender), and so Taureans may be drawn to work that champions women's interests, causes, and rights. It's also important for Taureans to feel they're working toward something that matters to them. They can really build something solid through their efforts, though if they can't see the point, it will be much more difficult for them to maintain motivation. Janet Jackson, a singer, dancer, and Taurus, said, "If I wasn't singing, I'd probably be an accountant." I find the juxtaposition interesting in relation to something Harry S. Truman, the thirty-third U.S. president and a Taurus, said: "If I hadn't been President of the United States, I probably would have ended up a piano player in a bawdy house." Both

Jackson and Truman, each a well-known Taurus in different positions at different times in history, said if they weren't pursuing their profession, they'd be doing something seemingly on the opposite end of the spectrum but still equally Taurean in its own right. With Janet—if not music, then finance; with Truman, if not being entrusted with one of the highest responsibilities, then music. Both encapsulate the full essence of their sun sign, Taurus.

Taurus has a fascination with value and consequently money. On a nine-hour international flight, I was in admiration of the attendants' ability to remain cheerful while serving two meals, including cleanup, in tight quarters, all while zipping across time zones. I then caught myself thinking, "They must get paid well." And then, "Oh, God, I hope they get paid well!" Believing proper compensation plays a large part in the acknowledgment of a job well done, a Taurus will always see the value in compensation that matches the time and effort. Also, this is not the first time I've caught myself in that thought, in true Taurus fashion. I am always curious about what people do and the value attached to it—it's an innate curiosity about how people earn and then what they decide to do. A big part of Taurus's sense of security is tied to these concepts, and so I suppose it's no surprise my Taurean instincts go there.

Taureans are not afraid of hard work whether it is in the arts or at a bank. They give it their all and quite enjoy it if they can see the value in what they're doing. There is a specific kind of pleasure that comes from exerting yourself and getting to see the fruits of your labor. Taureans are deliberate about how and when they spend their energy. You've probably seen mentions on the Internet about Taureans being lazy. I've never fully bought into that, as it's a little too vague; I think this stereotype may have more to do with motivation than with sheer laziness. Why should Taureans budge from a comfy seat if they don't see the value of the effort? When they do decide to commit, they're all in, and they give their fullest—and they'll also require the rest that is their due once they're done. A Taurus can't be rushed once they sit down to relax. Everything has its time and purpose when it comes to this sign.

A Taurus at work is a doer. They like to know what's expected of them and then get to it. Taureans also tend to do well under pressure and take challenges in stride; they're steady by nature, and so it takes quite a lot to unsettle them. A Taurean tends to be a steadfast force in the workplace and a calming presence. I have a dear friend, Linda, a Capricorn and private chef, whom I've helped on some very high-end, high-stress intimate dinners and parties over the years. I felt so much pride when she told me I was one of her favorite friends to have help because she found my presence in those situations calming; even when there was chaos or demanding clients, I managed to stay steady as a rock. I take so much pride in this compliment! This is not to say we Taureans never get stressed, but it's fair to say that when we do get stressed, we tend to dig in and root down, which definitely has an anchoring effect.

Taurus is a security-centered sign. Change is not their favorite thing in the world, as it may threaten to rock the boat of their precious stability. They like to know where their paycheck is coming from, how much, and how frequently. For this reason they prefer jobs that have stability and room to grow, with a consistent and reliable paycheck. Truth be told, they'll do whatever they set their minds to, though jobs at which variables are flexible, such as sales or working on commission, are not likely to be their first choice. Taking big risks regularly in their business affairs is not for them.

A Taurus in a senior position makes for a fair boss. They are clear and direct, and they expect you to do what you've said you will do. They are patient and prefer that things be done well and so are willing to invest time and money in your training. They'll expect you to be on time, give your very best, and follow through. They appreciate honest, genuine people and want them on their team.

Taureans in junior positions won't mind answering to their superiors. They understand that it takes time to build a career and reach the higher ranks. They're happy to launch right into their assignments and will work hard to earn their way up. Taureans do well when they have a clear understanding of what's expected of them, while unclear direction may cause frustration and lead to doubts about their superior's judgment.

Taurus employees are diligent and will accomplish every task asked of them, but once they find their routine, they won't appreciate it being changed much. It's true that they can be stubborn and set in their ways: If it works, why change it? It's unlikely that they will be persuaded to change easily. It has to be their idea, so provide them with clear-cut facts and a little time and they'll soon come around.

TAURUS

in School

"The most effective way to do it, is to do it."

—AMELIA EARHART, AVIATION PIONEER, AUTHOR, AND
TAURUS RISING WITH SUN IN LEO, BORN JULY 24

I n school, Taurus children have an even-keeled, steady approach to learning. They understand that they'll be given lessons and tasks within certain parameters, and they don't mind this, as what is expected of them will be obvious and they prefer this kind of clarity. They are determined and diligent; it may take them longer than their peers to complete their assignments, but their work gets done none-theless, and they are quite thorough. They won't be satisfied with turning in incomplete work, because they really want to do well and strive to put in the effort and time. They pride themselves on doing high-quality work.

The most challenging part for a Taurus is usually time constraints. If an assignment has a tight deadline, for example, or when they are taking a timed test, Taurean students may become stressed out, as they much prefer to move at their own pace. Adjusting to fit the system in this way can be difficult for them. They also do well with hands-on learning, since being able to lose themselves in an immersive experience makes sense to them. Therefore, field trips, recess, gym, theater, and band class may be some of their favorites as they allow them to use their bodies to connect to their learning experience. They also enjoy extra-curricular activities that allow them to do the same things, such as dance class and vocal coaching, especially if the school schedule doesn't offer much opportunity to engage physically throughout the day.

Later in life, when Taureans decide they might like to pursue higher levels of study, whether it is college or other serious training programs to hone a skill, they will do so with careful and thoughtful consideration. They weigh all the options. It's not something they go into lightly, as they value their time and resources (i.e., money) and want to be sure it's the next right step. They know that once they commit, they are all in, 110 percent.

They may be drawn to pursue an education in the arts, with a focus on vocal performance, dance, or even fine art or art history with the intention of working in a museum where they would be in charge of overseeing and organizing beautiful items. Taureans love to be surrounded by attractive things that carry special significance, without a doubt.

Many Taurus students may elect to go to culinary school to learn skills that enhance their adoration of food. Some may gravitate toward studying wine in hopes of becoming a sommelier, a profession that utilizes their heightened sense of taste and smell. Their love of nature may pull them to study agriculture or landscaping or even apprentice to a florist. Skills in the beauty and health realm are also something Taureans may be drawn to; costume design, for example, may be gratifying, since it allows them to work with textiles. Massage, aromatherapy, Reiki, and other bodywork modalities in the wellness realm also correspond well to Taurus sensibilities.

Taureans' grounded, practical nature means they would do well in the study of finance, money management, and even real estate. Once they decide on an area of study, they are sure to do well as their qualities of endurance mean they stick to what they start.

Although it may take Taureans longer to digest their studies, once they do, they retain the information and carry it with them always. A Taurus once told me her greatest accomplishment was completing her schooling, saying it took so long that it was a triumph to finish. To be clear, Taurus's slow and steady pace has nothing to do with lack of intelligence or laziness. They just take their time. (There are of course other factors to look at within your chart. In addition to your sun sign, you'll want to look to Mercury, as Mercury's sign and placement offer insight into your communication style as well as how you digest information. The signs on your third and ninth house cusps are also important, as together they correspond to how you relate to communications and learning from early on—third house—to higher education and your personal philosophies—ninth house.) Having said that, a Taurus simply can't be rushed with schooling—or anything else for that matter. They move at their own pace; that works for them. They're slow and methodical. As the old saying goes, slow and steady wins the race. This is why it's so important that they be interested and invested in their area of study. If they can't see the point or value, a lethargic resistance may set in that makes the task seem unbearably laborious even by their own standards—motivation will be hard to find. When motivation is there, though, they persist gladly. They need to find an area of study that really sparks joy within them. Once they do, they're unstoppable.

As I write this section on school, I'm reminded of my own college experience and how I came to live in New York City over fourteen years ago. As I mentioned earlier in this book, Taureans tend to have natural creative abilities, particularly when it comes to the voice, so let me tell you about my college experience. Well, when it came time to submit college applications, I painstakingly selected the handful of schools I would apply to on the basis of a few factors: all were state schools in Wisconsin, where I am from, but one. I chose one public school that was tough to get into but highly rated academically. I chose one that I knew I would get into and that would offer the experience of city living (which I desperately wanted, having grown up in a small town), one surefire getting-in-without-having-to-think-about-it school, and one dream school: a little theater conservatory called the American Musical and

Dramatic Academy (AMDA) in New York City. Looking back, applying to four schools seems a bit excessive, but hey, I wanted options.

I auditioned for AMDA in Chicago when they did their annual traveling audition rounds for the upcoming semester. My mom and I traveled the two hours south to Chicago and made an event of it by renting a hotel room—it was a special occasion. I belted my lungs out to prep in that little hotel room until our neighbor told me to cool it. I had made my decision, I'd prepared well, and I would follow through to the best of my ability with all my might. If I didn't get into AMDA, it would not be because I didn't try with all that I had.

Once in the audition room, I was nervous but jumped in and lost myself in the music. I did a great job and knew it but also knew that the competition was immense and fierce. When my acceptance letter came, I could hardly contain myself—I had gotten in! Just to clarify, I am not someone who trained from an early age to be a performer or who comes from a family line of performers. If anything,

I started formal training late by beginning in middle school. I made the most of my audition for school by tapping into the flow of my natural abilities: what has always been there and always will be for a Taurus Sun. A big part of what resonated and worked for me during my time at AMDA, aside from honing my natural Taurean abilities, was that it was a fully immersive experience. We were dancing, acting out scenes, and belting out ballads every single day in front of our peers as well as top talent in New York City—our teachers. Intimidating, yes. Rewarding, also yes. Unstoppable, for sure.

Give Taureans a duty and a deadline and we will rise to the occasion. For this reason, the conservatory-style school format worked well for me. I knew what was expected, and I had to commit physically to getting it done each day. Taurus blossoms though hands-on learning—embodiment combined with repetition of the study really helps it stick. When my editor, Kate, approached me about writing this book, Taurus, as part of the zodiac series with Sterling Ethos, I was thrilled. I thought of how great it would be to write my own sun sign as an opportunity to reflect on my personal experiences as a Taurus in order to share with you what it really means to live as the embodiment of a Taurus. I was right: it has been so much fun to reflect in this way.

TAURUS

in Daily Life

"Just be what you are. And I try to be my best self and be what I am and knowing what I am and be satisfied with that. And if people don't know it, maybe they'll eventually know it."

—CORETTA SCOTT KING, AUTHOR, ACTIVIST, CIVIL RIGHTS LEADER, AND TAURUS SUN, BORN APRIL 27

TAURUS DATES:

April 20–May 20

TAURUS KEY CONCEPT:

I Have

TAURUS SYMBOL:

The Bull   ♉

TAURUS RULING PLANET:

Venus   ♀

TAURUS MODALITY:

Fixed

TAURUS ELEMENT:

Earth

TAURUS HOUSE:

Second

TAURUS POSITIVE/ NEGATIVE CORRELATION:

Negative, Feminine

TAURUS IN THE BODY:

Neck
Throat
Vocal cords
Thyroid
Ears

TAURUS FLORA + FAUNA:

Rose
Poppy
Daisy
Foxglove
Cypress tree
Apple tree
Cattle

TAURUS METAL + GEMSTONE:

Copper
Emerald

Sensual
Stable
Reliable
Diligent
Loyal
Sensory
Security-oriented
Patient
Warmhearted
Loving
Prosperous
Calm
Deliberate
Materialistic
Persevering
Retentive

Physical
Affectionate
Steadfast
Stubborn
Immovable
Values-oriented
Consistent
Thorough
Attentive
Retentive

TAURUS COLORS:

Light blue
Green
Pink
Earth tones
Pastel shades

For Taureans, daily life and routines will always include pleasing sensory experiences. Incorporating plenty of sleep, regular mealtimes with delicious options (wilted lettuce and underripe tomatoes will not do), walks in nature, stimulating color, a luxuriously scented candle at the office or at home, fun music, and a comfy place to sit will ensure that they are happy but also at their peak of productivity. They are highly attuned to their surroundings, and so loud noise, proximity to the garbage can, stiff furniture, lack of nature, and general disorder in their environment will hinder their sense of well-being.

Venus is the planet that governs Taurus, and so Taureans are extra sensitive to it's movements. Venus moves through each sign of the zodiac for approximately three and a half weeks at a time and retrogrades every eighteen months for about six weeks. These will be key times to note on your calendar if you're a Taurus or have Taurus rising as you (and Libra, also ruled by Venus) will feel the effect of these shifts more than people of the other signs. It's also advisable for all signs to avoid launching a business, making important financial decisions, or experimenting with anything beauty-related, such as cosmetic surgery or drastic changes to one's appearance, while Venus is retrograde. Retrograde planets are not at their full power, and with Venus ruling beauty, social exchange, and money, initiations begun while Venus is retrograde are likely to have disappointing and unfruitful results.

THE TAURUS HOME

If you're invited to a Taurus's home, it is likely that you will be offered something delicious to nibble on, some rose-infused tea, or a glass of rosé wine. After being welcomed into a well-kept living room, you'll find the perfect spot to take a seat. Perhaps on a well-built yet comfy couch next to a soft throw blanket. The beautifully curated rooms in the house may sport muted tones of blue and green and colors you'd find in nature, such as taupe. There is sure to be lovely art adorning the walls and the strains of some pleasant melody drifting across the room from the stereo.

The influence of Venus will be obvious in a Taurus home. It will be visually appealing, comfortable, and a space you'll thoroughly enjoy being in, so much so that you'll probably lose your sense of time because it's easy to unwind in such a comfortable space. You'll certainly find plant life as well, whether it's a lush garden in the backyard or, if they're apartment-bound, lots of plants dotting any clear surface and of course a vase of fresh flowers. If you need to bring a housewarming gift for a Taurus, you can't lose with items that delight the senses—pick up some cocoa-dusted truffles, pale pink roses, or a hardy green plant in a beautiful pot.

TAURUS FASHION

Taurus colors are light blues and greens and pink, as well as colors that correlate with nature and pastel shades in general. When it comes to fashion, Taureans generally adore well-made items. They'd much rather have a handful of beautifully made pieces than a closet full of cheap wares that will last only for a season. They may own special pieces that are made to last in breathable, comfortable fabrics such as cotton and linen or soft luxurious cashmere in beautiful layerable shades that together build an outfit that is truly pleasing to the eye. Their aesthetic won't be the flashiest at the party, but it will be flattering and likely to prompt guests to say, "That's gorgeous. Where did you find it?" Taureans have a natural undeniable allure, and with Venus, the planet of love and grace, as their ruler, it makes sense.

TAURUS HEALTH

Each sign of the zodiac has an area of the body it's linked to. For Taurus, it's the neck, throat, vocal cords, thyroid, and ears. These areas of the body hold special significance for a Taurus. For this reason, Taureans may find that when under stress, they're more susceptible to sore throats than are the other signs. In moments of stress, Taureans may find grounding exercises such as yoga, exercise, earthing (placing bare feet and hands on the ground outdoors), and aromatherapy helpful—anything that connects them back to nature.

NEGATIVE AND POSITIVE

All signs are either positive/masculine (the air and fire signs, traditionally ruling the odd-numbered houses of the twelve houses) or negative/feminine (the earth and water signs, traditionally ruling the even-numbered houses of the twelve houses). This does not mean positive/negative as in "good or bad," and feminine/masculine is not about gender but rather about energetic expression of the sign. We all carry each of these qualities—positive, negative, feminine, and masculine—within us. They indicate which signs are thought- and action-oriented and more outwardly expressive, yang energies (positive/masculine) and which are more inward-turning, reflective, and related to the manifestation and growth of our ideas, yin energy (negative/feminine). Taurus is the first of the negative/feminine signs, and it is fertile ground for growth once we have an idea of what we're after. It's the Taurus side of ourselves that conspires to manifest our inner thoughts into an actual reality.

SOCIAL TAURUS

At first impression some may think the Taurus in the group is shy, but that is not necessarily true. However, there is some truth to the idea that Taureans are not the most talkative of the bunch (assuming they don't have other strong indicators of this within their birth charts, such as a strong

Gemini or Sagittarius influence, for example). This is the case because they prefer to take their time to observe the person or situation at hand, to be sure they fully understand and then form a well-rounded idea or response, before sharing. So, while Taureans are perhaps quieter than other signs, when they do share, it's clear and thought out and usually makes a lot of sense.

Common sense is not something Taureans lack. Their nature is practical, sensible, and to the point—there won't be a lot of fluff encasing what they have to say. Taurus actor Cate Blanchett in response to an interview question about people's need to share on social media said it best: "I'm of the opinion that it's okay to be silent, to not speak if you don't have anything to say."

In their free time, Taureans enjoy being outdoors, hitting up the farmers' market, treating themselves at the spa, gardening, and honing their culinary skills by taking a fun cooking or wine-tasting class. They also adore travel that includes exceptional food experiences, the opportunity to explore wine regions, and breathtaking nature destinations.

TAURUS

I was visiting with friends one evening when we got to discussing a *New York Times* article titled "To Fall in Love with Anyone, Do This." The article explains that psychologist Arthur Aron came up with a series of thirty-six questions meant to be relationship-building. The topic came up because my friend Lauren had all thirty-six questions, handwritten, in her purse so that she would be prepared for a conversation about the article should the right moment strike—such a good little Virgo!

We asked each other a few, one being "Your house, containing everything you own, catches fire. After saving your loved ones and pets, you have time to safely make a final dash to save any one item. What would it be? Why?" A Taurus at the table shared that she would save her father's gold wedding band, which she would already be wearing as she rarely takes it off, as well as his guitar. Her father passed when she was a baby, and though she did not get to know him, she treasured those two items left to her in memory of him. The ring and guitar are valuable in their own right, but the value of what they represent to her is priceless. It struck me how true this rings for a Taurus. These items are high-quality of course, but more importantly, they have sentimental value attached to them, and that makes them particularly special.

Another question on the list was "Describe your perfect day." My fellow Taurus described a day with breakfast first thing, a nice long bike ride, and then a second breakfast. Quite right, Taurus, quite right. I laughed when I heard this, because the first thing that came to mind was a running tradition with a dear friend who sends me a quote from the movie *Miss Congeniality* every year on April 25, my birthday. In it, a judge in a beauty pageant asks, "Miss Rhode Island, please describe your idea of a perfect date." Cheryl, the contestant from Rhode Island, responds, "That's a tough one. I'd have to say April 25. Because it's not too hot, not too cold, all you need is a light jacket." April 25 is my birthday, falling early in Taurus season, and to be honest, I do think it is the perfect date. Maybe it's the season, finally warm with spring foliage in the northern hemisphere, or maybe it's my natural sentiment to love the warmth of attention during that time. With Venus as their ruling planet, Taureans are set up to thoroughly enjoy luxuriating and being appreciated on their birthday, or if they're like me, they may enjoy doing so throughout their entire *birthday month*. Taureans don't mind having a reason to treat themselves.

If I had to describe a perfect day, though, it would be similar to my friend's: nature without a doubt, probably the ocean or a spot with some spongy green grass and flowers nearby, fresh air, killer snacks, and time with loved ones, then later maybe some live music or a Broadway show—and of course a second breakfast.

TAURUS SENSITIVITIES

Taurus senses are finely tuned. This is one of Taureans' greatest gifts, but at times, this quality can work against them. They'll go weak at the allure of your floral perfume or a home-cooked meal and can have a spiritual experience listening to their favorite song in the car. The flip side is that they'll also be more sensitive than most to loud noises and foul odors. (I once smelled my neighbor changing their baby's diaper in the apartment below—no, I'm not kidding. My partner, a Leo, was totally oblivious to it.) They'll be especially grumpy if they have not had enough sleep or it's been too long since their last meal. They function best on plenty of sleep and regular meals. As Linda Goodman hilariously said of Taurus in her bestselling book *Sun Signs* (Macmillan 1972), "Flat hamburgers and bland pea soup leave her emotionally cold." It's just par for the course—those Taurean senses are heightened for better or worse.

TAURUS

in the World

"Ability may get you to the top, but it takes character to keep you there."

—Stevie Wonder, singer, songwriter, musician, record producer, and Taurus Sun, born May 13

Each sign in union with its planetary ruler plays a distinctive role within the zodiac. We need all the parts, and all the parts are within us. The role of Taurus is to remind us to ground ourselves in the present moment. Taurus reminds us that we are creatures of the Earth, having an earthly experience. This sign, along with its ruling planet, Venus, teaches us to plan thoughtfully in the now so that we may build a nest egg for the future and of course to submerge ourselves fully in the sensory delights the world has to offer. It's the part of ourselves we tap into to create, make art, dance, and sing, eat well, and love deeply and with intention. Without Taurus, how would we know how to establish strong roots from which to grow our lives? There is much joy to be found through exploring the Taurean part of your chart. Taureans do what they say they're going to do. Their follow-through is strong. The world would be a much sadder place without the Taureans' stable, soft, and enduring Venusian influence. I mean, could you imagine a world without music? Art? Lasting relationships? No thanks. Our Taurean companions are steady and good-humored forces in our lives, as well as out in the world at large.

The deeper you dive into your studies to broaden your understanding of astrology, the more you will begin to see its connection to mythology all around you. From the constellation-speckled ceiling of Grand Central Terminal in New York City to the well-known car company Saturn Corporation; or Mars Inc., known for your favorite candy bars, snacks, and pet foods; to popular music—"Life on Mars?" by David Bowie, or how about "There's a Moon in the Sky (Called the Moon)" by the B-52s (check out the lyrics for some fun planetary shout-outs)—astrological imagery is all around us.

It's clear to see astrology's impact and the way it permeates our culture. Some confuse astrology with a belief system or think of astrology as a religion in and of itself, but that is not the case. Astrology in fact has the capacity to enhance those things. It does not negate them. It is the study of planetary cycles, of nature, using math—specifically geometry—to understand how those cycles affect our daily lives and the world at large. It teaches us how to work more consciously with those patterns to achieve greater harmony in our lives. I like to say it's a bit like the weather:

you don't believe in the weather, it just is. You can plan for the weather . . . or not. Either way it will be there.

Astrology is a tool, accessible to all, so why not add it to your tool belt and plan for success? At the very least, it may help you navigate times of discord with a little more ease. Humans have been using astrology nearly since the beginning of time, and somehow it's managed to make it this far. If it didn't work, I personally think it would not have managed to stick around for so long. So you see, astrology itself is not a belief system or a religion but a study of nature—specifically planetary cycles—that coexists in combination with your other studies and personal experiences to enrich your life even further.

The astrologer Susan Miller, a devout Catholic, told me she believes God created astrology to help us navigate our lives. She said, "Consider nature—everything has a reason, why would the planets be any different?" I couldn't agree more. I do believe in something greater than ourselves: God in you and me, animals and nature, our higher-self, the universe. It is part of creation like everything else, and everything is connected. Astrology is one lens of many through which we can navigate the world. If it is helpful, use it! If you don't find it helpful, there are millions of other lenses to explore. However, I would encourage you to dig a little deeper and learn more about astrology's roots and the fundamentals of how it works before dismissing it. Everyone is a skeptic until they dig deeper, and rightfully so. Take a class, read books, and schedule a reading with an astrologer. I think you'll be pleasantly surprised at how your perspective broadens. Mine did! Astrology really helped me understand key parts of myself in profound and healing ways, so much so that it altered my career path—and now here I sit, writing this book about Taurus.

TAURUS IN POPULAR CULTURE

Curious about where to look for Taurus in popular culture? Take a look at the well-known Taurus Suns and Taurus risings below. Besides being really fun, it's also interesting to see the common threads they all may share.

Well-Known Taurus Suns

Adele

Jessica Alba

Wes Anderson

Will Arnett

Fred Astaire

David Beckham

Irving Berlin

Cate Blanchett

Bono

Pierce Brosnan

James Brown

Aidy Bryant

Carol Burnett

Busta Rhymes

Catherine the Great

Cher

Kelly Clarkson

George Clooney

Stephen Colbert

Sofia Coppola

Bing Crosby

Penélope Cruz

Salvador Dalí

Bobby Darin*

Rosario Dawson

Sandra Dee

Kirsten Dunst

Queen Elizabeth II

*Denotes Taurus Sun with Taurus rising, or a Double Taurus—meaning they are extra-true to the qualities of their sign, Taurus.

Duke Ellington

Nora Ephron

Tina Fey

Ella Fitzgerald

Sigmund Freud

Jean Paul Gaultier

Crispin Glover*

Gigi Hadid*

Tony Hawk

Audrey Hepburn

Katharine Hepburn

Iggy Pop

Enrique Iglesias

Janet Jackson

Billy Joel

Dwayne Johnson, the Rock

Grace Jones

Coretta Scott King

Liberace

Lizzo

George Lucas*

Patti Lupone

Shirley MacLaine

Malcolm X

Rami Malek

Master P

Tim McGraw

Meek Mill

Michael Moore

Willie Nelson

Jack Nicholson

John Oliver

Robert Oppenheimer

Roy Orbison

Al Pacino

Bettie Page

Michelle Pfeiffer

Dennis Rodman

Travis Scott

Jerry Seinfeld

William Shakespeare

Robert Smith

Sam Smith

George Strait

Barbra Streisand

Channing Tatum

Shirley Temple

Donatella Versace*

Robert Penn Warren

August Wilson

Stevie Wonder

Renée Zellweger

Mark Zuckerberg

Well-Known Taurus Risings*

Luis Walter Alvarez
(Gemini Sun)

Halle Berry (Leo Sun)

Julian Bond
(Capricorn Sun)

Charles Bukowski
(Leo Sun)

Jean Cocteau (Cancer Sun)

Billy Crystal (Pisces Sun)

Angela Davis
(Aquarius Sun)

Amelia Earhart (Leo Sun)

Mia Farrow (Aquarius Sun)

Steve Forbes (Cancer Sun)

Robert F. Kennedy
(Scorpio Sun)

Martin Luther King, Jr.
(Capricorn Sun)

David Letterman
(Aries Sun)

George R. R. Martin
(Virgo Sun)

Herman Melville (Leo Sun)

Liza Minnelli (Pisces Sun)

Charley Pride (Pisces Sun)

Queen Latifah (Pisces Sun)

Toni Morrison
(Aquarius Sun)

*NOTE: The rising sign is an extremely important placement in your natal horoscope; you can read the books in this series and your favorite horoscope columns for both your sun sign and your rising sign. Your rising sign can be calculated only by using your exact birth time. See the introduction to this book for more information. All Taurus risings listed here have a Rodden Rating of either A or AA.

Wayne Newton (Aries Sun)

Issa Rae (Capricorn Sun)

Bonnie Raitt (Scorpio Sun)

Fred Rogers (Pisces Sun)

Tracee Ellis Ross
   (Scorpio Sun)

Carl Sagan (Scorpio Sun)

Elliott Smith (Leo Sun)

Snoop Dogg (Libra Sun)

Dionne Warwick
   (Sagittarius Sun)

Sigourney Weaver
   (Libra Sun)

Mae West (Leo Sun)

Serena Williams
   (Libra Sun)

Brian Wilson (Gemini Sun)

TAURUS

CONCLUSION

"Success isn't always about greatness. It's about consistency. Consistent, hard work leads to success. Greatness will come."

– DWAYNE JOHNSON, THE ROCK, ACTOR, PRODUCER, PROFESSIONAL WRESTLER, AND TAURUS SUN, BORN MAY 2

Astrology opens our perceptions to a world brimming with potential within ourselves and also within each person in our lives, extending outward into the world. It broadens our view, enables us to see a situation from a new angle, and is a source of great compassion as it increases our empathy for not only our own situation but also the situations of the people around us, as well as offering invaluable insight into current events.

As you now know, astrology is much bigger than any one sign alone; its true value lies in the understanding of the sum of all of its parts. Each sign of the zodiac holds special significance in and of itself, but no one sign is better than any other, just as no one person is an island. As I said in the introduction to this book, "As above, so below—as within, so without." We are intrinsically linked to all of nature. We each have a responsibility to ourselves to strive to be the best we can be, and that has a reverb effect that extends much farther than ourselves. There is a dignity and great responsibility within the study and practice of astrology, my hope is that you will take this to heart and continue to expand your understanding.

The ancients were clearly on to something, as we still use astrology to inform greater understanding today after thousands of years. From its early beginnings in Mesopotamia to modern times, astrology has persisted because it works. Astrology is not predestination or a religion but rather a tool to help us navigate our lives and make more conscious decisions that are based on our unique challenges and strengths in any situation. We have free will and choose how to participate with the cosmic climate every step of the way. When you begin to study and use astrology in practice, that is when it really comes alive, and you reap the benefits within your life. It takes some time and commitment to learn, as astrology is a complex study, but I can assure you from my own experience that it's worth it! In fact, I never in a million years thought I would be working as a professional astrologer. Years ago a friend suggested that I take my now mentor Rebecca Gordon's beginner astrology course, and it was all over from there. It's true that astrology finds you.

If you are curious, if astrology's concepts stir excitement within you, keep going, keep learning, commit, and really go for it! I think each of us is a skeptic, and rightfully so, until we take the time to learn and see how astrology actually works. Astrology is the study of planetary cycles and possibility, an exploration of the synergy at play between the sun, the other luminary—the moon of course, all eight planets, and all twelve signs of the zodiac, as well as the twelve houses that the planets and the signs of the zodiac fall within. All parts must be integrated to best understand the whole. Most are aware of sun sign astrology, horoscopes in the paper, for example, and for good reason—the sun plays an extremely important role within our personal astrology and is the base of our solar chart. It's the core of who we are, but the scope of astrology in fact stretches much farther beyond your sun sign alone. Learning about your personal astrology will open a world of opportunity to you. The natal chart, based on your exact birth information is completely unique to you, your cosmic fingerprint. It will reveal intimate details such as your rising sign, as well as your sun, moon, and planetary placements within the signs and houses. The inner planets relate to your personality (Mercury, Venus, Mars)—the midplanets, Jupiter and Saturn, affect trends of the time—and your outer planetary placements (Uranus, Neptune, Pluto)—relate to generational influences. The outer planets move very slowly, staying in one sign for years at a time, and for this reason have a generational influence, whereas the inner planets make their trip around the sun quickly, thus change sign more frequently, and so relate more to our nuanced personalities in studying a natal chart. These factors are also the reason why you can meet another Taurus who has much different characteristics than you do but still has a similar guiding principle and sense of purpose.

It's important to integrate the chart as a whole in addition to learning about your sun sign. Also, if you have your birth time, you can calculate your chart through many free resources online. You will need your birth date, including the year; your exact time of birth; and your birth location. You will be prompted to enter your birth information; these sites will tell you what sign was rising on Earth's eastern horizon when you were born. The rising sign is also known as the ascendant (ASC). If you're unsure of your birth time, flip back to the introduction to this book, where I give some handy ways to procure it. Once you know your rising sign, or sign on your ascendant, be sure to read the book in this series for that sign as well. You can also read your favorite horoscope column for both your sun and rising signs, and I hope you do! You'll get a much better idea of the big picture when you do.

Taureans are intrinsically linked to the planet Venus; they are some of the most affectionate, genuine, and reliable people you could ever hope to know. Right from the beginning straight through to the end, from childhood to adulthood, in all facets of life, it's clear that Taurus is a sensual, stable, loyal, and calming force through and through. Want to enjoy life's pleasures more? Date a Taurus. Want someone to stand by you with a steadfastness that verges on the spiritual? Befriend a Taurus. Want someone you can trust completely to help build your business into a solid empire? Hire a Taurus. My hope is that through reading this book on Taurus you now have a deeper understanding of Taureans' nature, what drives them, and how to best utilize their natural gifts at work, in love, and in living life to the fullest.

You picked up this book and made the decision to expand your knowledge of Taurus in all its beautiful intricacies, so that is a great start! I hope you'll explore the other eleven books in this series as well, rounding out your understanding of the entire zodiac for the best results. The more we actively invest in learning about ourselves and one another and in experiences outside of our own, the more we foster an environment for compassion and understanding to thrive. This has a unifying ripple effect within our closest relationships, our community, our city, state, country, across the world, and beyond. As the spiritual teacher Ram Dass said, "We're all just walking each other home." I thank you with all my heart for taking the time to read this book.

NOTES

INTRODUCTION

Page 13   "There is a series of sacred texts . . ." Hermetica. (Last updated January 10, 2019, at 12:36 UTC.) In Wikipedia. Retrieved June 12, 2019, from https://en.wikipedia.org/wiki/Hermetica.

Page 13   Ibid. Hermes Trismegistus. (Last updated May 12, 2019, at 09:50 UTC.) In Wikipedia. Retrieved June 12, 2019, from https://en.wikipedia.org/wiki/Hermes_Trismegistus.

Page 13   "Astrologer and author Betty Lundsted . . ." Lundsted, Betty, Astrological Insights into Personality. Berwick, ME: Ibis Press, 2004.

CHAPTER 7

Page 99   "Taurus actor Cate Blanchett in . . ." Interview magazine (November 23, 2008), "Cate Blanchett." Accessed June 20, 2019, from https://www.interviewmagazine.com/film/cate-blanchett.

BIBLIOGRAPHY

The materials listed below have been influential for me. If you are curious about taking your understanding of astrology further, I highly recommend adding these resources to your bookshelf.

Bills, Rex E., The Rulership Book. Tempe, AZ: American Federation of Astrologers, 2007.

Goodman, Linda, Sun Signs. London: Pan Macmillan, 1972.

Hand, Robert, Planets in Youth. Westchester, PA: Schiffer, 1997.

Lundsted, Betty, Astrological Insights into Personality. Berwick, ME: Ibis Press, 2004.

Miller, Susan, Planets and Possibilities. New York: Grand Central Publishing, 2001.

Parker, Julia, and Derek Parker, Parkers' Astrology: The Essential Guide to Using Astrology in Your Daily Life. New York: Dorling Kindersley, 1994.

Sasportas, Howard, The Twelve Houses. London: Harper Collins, 1985.

ACKNOWLEDGMENTS

Some thanks are in order, for I could have never gotten to where I am today without my inner circle of exceptional people. Thanks to my family: mom Ella and brother Kevin, both Virgos; Leo sister Ea and dad Kevin; my inspiring niece Unity, an Aquarius; as well as a lifelong chosen family member, Lorna, the sweetest Cancer—thank you for your unwavering love and support, for encouraging me to follow my heart's calling, whether it be to acting school in New York City or becoming an astrologer; you have always urged me to dream big and then reach a little farther still, and I love you so much. Cassie, lifelong Taurean bestie and chosen sister, you brighten my life. My partner Scott, a Leo, thank you for your big heart, enduring belief in me, and for building me up always—you are a dream come true. Rebecca Gordon, Virgo extraordinaire! I thank my lucky stars our paths crossed, my mentor, teacher, friend, and ultimate cheerleader; I am forever grateful to you for introducing me to the depths of astrology. Susan Miller, the Queen, whose sign I will never share—promise! Thank you for your encouragement, wisdom, and guidance—your wealth of astrological and business knowledge has been invaluable; you are a guardian angel sent from above. My Capricorn editor, Kate Zimmermann, I am so grateful for your guidance and kindness. You invited me to be a part of this wonderful series and the Sterling Ethos family. What an honor—thank you, thank you, thank you. To every teacher I've had along the way, my astro family, my theater family, my NYC family, NYC itself (because let's be real, living in NYC is one of the biggest teachers you could ever imagine), you mean the world to me, you've shaped me, you inspire me to be the best version of myself. I am grateful for you every day.

You are each one in a million. How did I get so lucky? My love and respect for you are boundless. Thank you from the bottom of my heart.

TAURUS

INDEX

ABOUT THE AUTHOR

COURTNEY O'REILLY is a Taurus and a New York City–based astrologer and founder of Vibrant Soul Astrology. Her mentors include Rebecca Gordon of Rebecca Gordon Astrology and the world-renowned astrologer and founder of AstrologyZone.com, Susan Miller. Courtney has been featured in such publications as *Women's Health, The Dispatch,* and *Well+Good* and has worked with partners that include Planned Parenthood, Capsule, and Garmentory. She offers in-depth one-on-one personal readings and fun mini-reading events and is available for private event booking. Please say hi; Courtney would love to hear from you. Keep in touch by emailing courtney@vibrantsoul astrology.com and following her at vibrantsoulastrology .com as well as following her on Instagram and Facebook at @vibrantsoulastrology for all the latest astrology news.